LOADING...

Q: What did two tabs of acid Saturday morning
   teach you?

A: That we are _all_ borne of irresponsible parents.

PLAY ▶

an

INFINITY AWAITS!

episode

SP

Primary Objective:

THE
MONKEY-BANANA
REDUCTION

Side Quest:

AN
INCONSEQUENTIAL
EXPLOIT
OF
KAPITÄN SCHADENFREUDE

"The Lumen Frame"

+/- FRAGMENTS

00:00:00

HEATHEN SHORTS
THEIR STORIES. OUR WAY.

Published in the good ole United States of America
by Heathen Shorts, an imprint of
Heathen Creative
P.O. Box 588
Point Pleasant, WV 25550-0588

Heathen Shorts are available at quantity discounts.
Bear witness to the yackety-yak and tomfoolery at:

heatheneditions.com

Social? Tag us! @heatheneditions
Photo? Tag it! #heathenedition #heathenshort

Caution: This _____ may alter your mind.

Heathen Short published January 8, 2026

Book and cover design by Watson Thomas

ISBN: 979-8-90075-008-8

HEATHEN SHORT #8
FIRST EDITION

phase one, in which monkey gets his banana*

"Are we in it? We're in it, aren't we? Yeah, okay, we're in it, we're here, here we are, here we go."

"It has begun."

"I might vomit."

"You should, then."

"But I don't want to."

"But you should."

"But I don't want to."

"It's telling you that whatever you ate for breakfast is going to interfere with the experience, so it has to go."

"Right, I'm with you, I just need to not see the biscuits and gravy again because I really like biscuits and gravy, but if I vomit biscuits and gravy, I'm not going to like biscuits and gravy for a while, and the biscuits and gravy that I had this morning was delicious and I don't want—I can't lose that right now, okay? They were good. Like, *really* good. And I need that good thing in my life. It's one of the good things, and the good things are few."

"Mm. This is going to be some trip."

"Do you hear <[The Monkeys]> or am I tripping?"

"Yes."

---

* Two monkeys riding nowhere, spending some monkey's hard-earned pay.

```
                              scan\\set
                          ±contextualize°
                              run\/loop
                              >identify
                              >extract
                              >interpret
                          logic//apply
                              >subsume
                          if|then = esc
                              .^resume
                              ~//∞
                              | pilot |



                              *¬query!
                          qudo swot
                          ¶__"frag"
                          gen\\rnd
                          if|then = view
                                    /
                                    \
√fragment:/20171204.1707_>>
                                    /
                                    \
                          load//data
                              scan\\set
                          ±contextualize°
                              run\/loop
                              >identify
                              >extract
                              >interpret
                          logic//apply
                              >subsume
                          if|then = esc
                              .^resume
                              ~//∞
                              | pilot |



                              *¬query!
                          qudo assemble
                          ¶__"expe"
                          gen\\rnd
```

And then you smoke and it's like
    the opacity of the facade is reduced,
    and now you can hear the rivets
    in the fuselage popping
      while the altimeter screams
        and chaos claws at the door—

what paces:
  the anxious man.
  the confined prisoner.
  the caged animal.

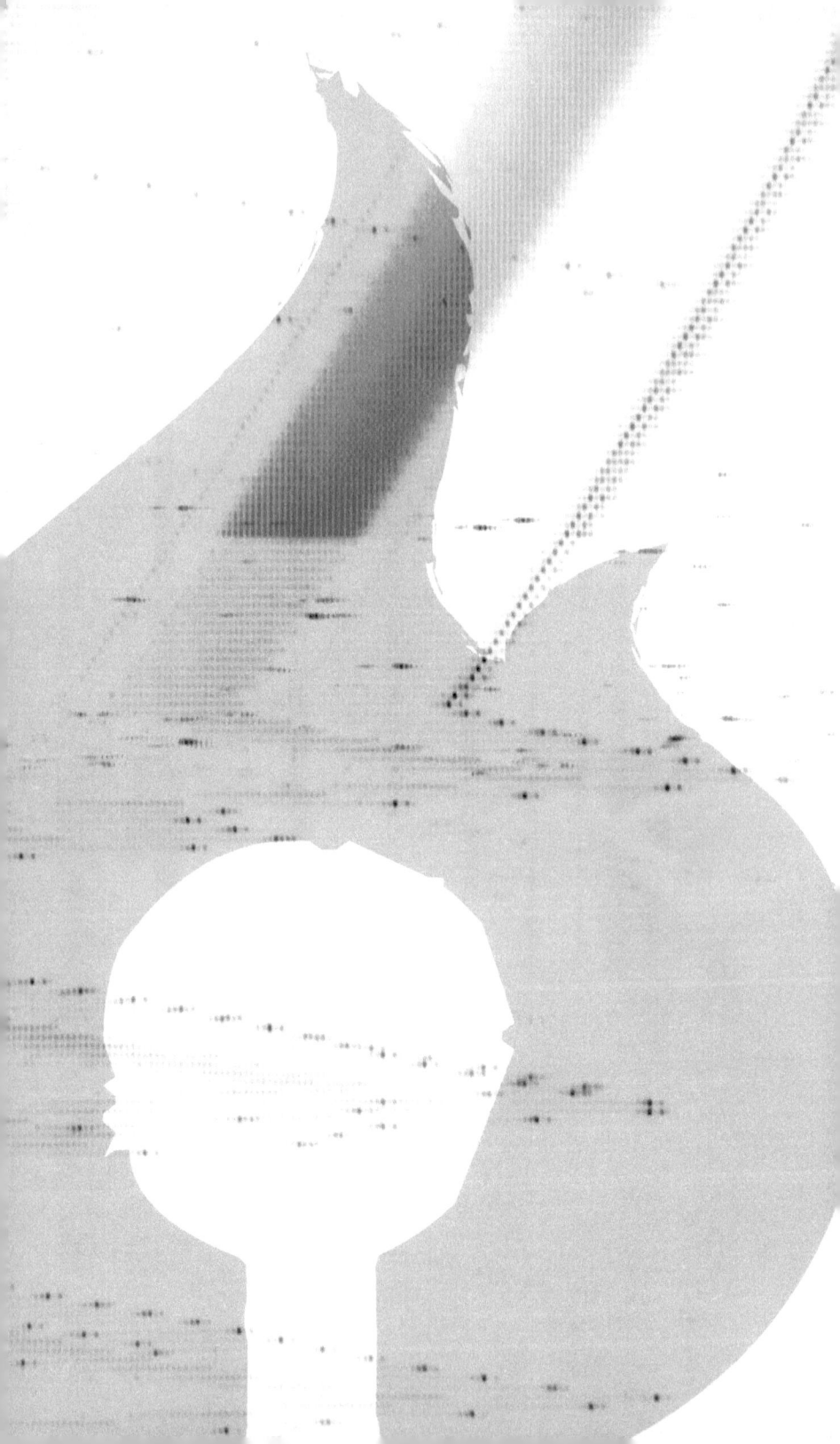

HEATHENRY
THOUGHTS ON THE TEXT

We'll hop straight to it with a transcribed excerpt from a recent conference call we Heathens had with Watson Thomas and Sheboygan Minnetonka:

Heathen Shorts: (terrible British accent) Oi! What's all this, then?

Watson Thomas: Well, here we go—

Sheboygan Minnetonka: Please speak with that accent for the rest of this call.

HS: (continued terrible British accent) Might be a bit too much, eh?

WT: Why are you—

SM: (laughs) This is great!

WT: —suddenly Australian?

HS: (terrible Australian accent) Cup-uh rooibos, eh?

SM: *Roy–bows?*

HS: Rooibos, eh?

WT: It's a tea. Looks like roo-e-boss?

SM: Oh! Wait, that's pronounced roy-bows?

HS: Rooibos, eh?

SM: Roy-bows. *Roy-bows.* Rooibos? It's like—

WT: See what you've done?!

SM: —you can't say it *without* sounding Australian. Rooibos. *Rooibos.*

HS: Rooibos, eh?

SM: *Rooibos, eh?*

HS: (laughs)

WT: (sighs) Monkeys all.

SM: (better Australian accent) Cup-uh rooibos, eh?

HS: (chuckles) You know what my grandpa would say?

WT: Dad-burn your hide?!

SM: (laughs) What?

HS: There ain't a boy here!

WT: Huh?

HS: He'd always say: one boy is all boy, two boys is half a boy, and three boys is no boy at all.

WT: Ah, I see—

SM: That's so true! Three boys equals trouble!

HS: And here we are . . .

HS: All right, so, Watson, for real this time: What's all this, then?

WT: "What does it all mean, all this shit I'm seein'?"

SM: (singing) *There's somethin' happenin' here—*

HS: I guess walk us through what we're about to, er—uh—what we're already experiencing as a reader?

WT: Okay, so, let me see if I can condense this as briefly as possible: acid trip, ego death, mind blown, life implodes (but not because of the preceding), then the Creative stopped creating.

HS: Why not because of the preceding?

WT: My life was already imploding. The LSD-induced ego death was . . . you know those whistler fireworks?

SM: Yeah! (whistles), then—(explosion noise).

WT: It was like that. The Brilliant White Light was the (explosion noise) of the implosion.

HS: And that's one of the Fragments?

WT: Yes. Its first line was how I described the ego death immediately after it happened, and, at the time, I knew exactly what that meant, but had absolutely no idea what I was saying (anyone familiar with the psychedelic experience will understand, maybe). It was—those were just the first words that came to me.

SM: Like a knee-jerk?

WT: Sort of? You know when someone hits you and the immediate, involuntary response is "Ow!" It was like—you know those rapid-fire montages in *Snatch*?

HS: Yes! Taxi, airplane, passport; boom-boom-boom—

WT: Imagine it like that: soaring through clouds, everything forgotten, even my name, me becomes I, Infinite Plane, Orb of Absolute Love, symbiosis, then I is me again and, "I have danced a cosmic dance, danced for eons."

SM: Sounds wild. Sign me up!

HS: Okay, so (whistles), then (explosion noise), and then the Creative stopped creating? Why?

WT: I feel like I'm skipping over a lot, but, essentially, because disconnect. I felt disconnected and I needed to disconnect and so I disconnected. I went from writing daily to not writing at all. Before, I was the guy who could fire off a 10,000 word email before lunch. After, I felt like a monkey in *2001: A Space Odyssey*.

HS: (laughs) How so?

WT: Well, you know how they're just fiddling with the bones and they don't understand them?

ends p. xx

HS: Yes?

SM: Bones?! You mean bananas!

WT: Ha! Well, replace the bones—sorry, *bananas*—with words. I was a monkey who didn't understand words. You know: picks up word, "HooHoo." (makes hammering noises)

HS: How long did the creative drought last?

WT: Almost three years.

SM: That seems quite a stretch.

HS: You didn't write *anything* during those three years?

WT: A little. Some poems. A few abandoned pieces. Nothing substantial until "A Conversation with Cassavetes."

HS: Which is the last part of this **Short**?

WT: Yes. We end where I began again.

HS: And that's not even substantial, right? It's just 1200 words.

WT: Right. But that was *the most* at the time.

HS: So that "conversation" with Cassavetes ignited something?

WT: In a way, yeah. It reignited the writing pilot light.

SM: And you were tripping when you wrote that?

WT: Technically, yes, I was still in a three-tab experience, but I was on the comedown, the gentle glide.

HS: So it's kind of a pseduo trip report?

WT: In some ways, yeah. Like the mention of voices, which is in no way schizo and in all ways my acid-brain having ∞ thoughts at once.

HS: Okay, so there's a re-ignition à la Cassavetes. How long before "The Monkey-Banana Reduction"?

WT: Almost two years. I spent most of that time wrestling with trying to figure out the writing style/mode that became/ produced "Monkey-Banana." There were a lot of false starts and many more abandoned pieces. I knew I had things to say, but didn't know how I wanted to say it, exactly, other than I knew I wanted it to replicate the psychedelic experience.

SM: Chaos.

WT: Yes. And that was the problem: How does one create, in literary form, the chaos of a psychedelic experience, but make it readable, make it entertaining, make it sincere, make it thought-provoking—make it personal and universal at the same time?

HS: Ah, there's a quote from Robert Hunter—

SM: Who's that?

HS: He was a lyricist for the Grateful Dead. I was listening to a retrospective on NPR after he passed in 2019, and in an interview he said, "If something is personal enough, there's a certain line where it becomes universal."

WT: Great quote, and very true.

SM: When you reduce everything to monkey/banana, then everything is universal.

WT: Exactly!

HS: So, what clicked? What broke the creative dam?

WT: When I started looping back to the *1984*/Orwell riff and **Head** in "Monkey-Banana." Before that, I kept struggling with how to create written fractals. The first time I circled back to those, I knew I had it. In that moment it was like being in the psychedelic experience—I could see infinity—and I knew it was working, where to go, what to write. At that time, all I could think to call what I had done was a fractal. It wasn't until later that I discovered the Jane Alison book *Meander, Spiral, Explode: Design and Pattern in Narrative*, which has a whole chapter devoted to fractals, which both fascinated me and made me laugh when I read it because I realized I had blindly but intuitively brute-forced my way into that narrative pattern.

HS: That's a great book. I read it after you mentioned it to me.

ends p. xx

WT: Yeah, anyone interested in alternative/experimental narrative structures should definitely read it.

HS: Okay, so, man—I have so many more questions, but I don't want to spoil anything . . . I guess let's skip to how you end "Cassavetes" and how that ties into the **Fragments** that you've collected here.

WT: Yeah, so I end "Cassavetes" literally with a setup, which both speaks to individual writing sessions, kind of like an allusion to that writing maxim 'end the session knowing where the next session will begin,' but it's also a **Short** setup for an **Original** payoff.

SM: I see what you did there!

WT: (laughs) And the **Fragments** in this **Short** are pieces of that larger work, tentatively entitled *Infinity Awaits? Amuse It!*

HS: Let's talk visual style. I see some elements carried over from *Propaganda*?[1]

WT: Yep, definitely. Working on that book gave me a lot of visual ideas that I've brought to this **Short**.

SM: That's not a book, that's a trip!

HS: (laughs) Yeah?

SM: It's wild how you weave the **Heathenry** throughout the entire book.

HS: That was the idea, to make the book a visual representation of trying to tune into a frequency, where you're reading Bernays' instruction/analysis on propaganda, while receiving our Heathen propaganda between its chapters. Like two books blending in a cross-frequency.

SM: Yeah, that shit is wild!

---

[1] *Propaganda* by Edward Bernays (Heathen Edition) now available, which was designed entirely by Watson Thomas.

HS: All right, so, Watson, I remember when I told you that we wanted to do this **Short,** you immediately said that we had to include Sheboygan's short. Why?

WT: Because monkeys and bananas.

SM: (laughs) Right?!

WT: I think our works are great complimentary pieces. Not just because of the monkeys and bananas, or because we're both "failed filmmakers" in our own ways, but because both pieces speak to the absurdity of this moment of ours, culturally. I'm riffing on consumerist materialism, Sheboygan's riffing on the perpetual cognitive dissonance of social media. Both, ultimately, have net negative consequences for the individual.

HS: And I'll take advantage of that segue way: Sheboygan, what was the inspiration for *Schadenfreude*?

SM: Some assholes.

HS: (laughs) Oh yeah?

SM: Yeah, some mentally-ill dude I haven't spoken to in years decided to rake me over the coals on social media for a decade-old unfinished short film that he wasn't a part of or even contributed to, and that trolling brought out more trolls, you know, people who never take creative risks themselves, but are quick to criticize other Creatives when they fail. If "Cassavetes" was a re-ignition of a writing pilot light for Watson, this trolling episode was someone leaving the gas on and KABOOM! for me.

HS: It definitely reads that way.

WT: Scathing, for sure.

HS: Those English subtitles, though.

WT: Right?!

SM: (laughs) Cranking that dissonance to eleven.

ends next p.

HS: Final thoughts?

SM: *Rooibos, eh?*

WT: Callback!

HS: Tea sounds good, actually.

WT: What's your favorite?

HS: Depends on my mood, and what I have on hand. I like variety, so I'm constantly trying new blends, but I like bold, black teas. I think my current favorite is Lapsang Souchong.

SM: Whosa whatsa?

HS: (laughs) It's a black tea smoke-dried over a pinewood or pine-needle fire.

SM: Say *whaaaaat*?

WT: What does *that* taste like?

HS: I call it the Scotch of teas.

WT: Oh!

SM: Sounds wild. Sign me up!

HS: It's campfire in a cup, and so good.

WT: There should be a Heathen tea.

HS: We've thought about it.

SM: Stop thinking, start doing!

WT: What were you thinking?

HS: Something bold, complex, and smooth. I'd want to use Lapsang for its smokiness, but add dark chocolate and tobacco into the mix.

SM: Tobacco?

HS: Yeah, I hate the way it tastes, but I love the way chewing tobacco smells. Bit of nostalgia, I think—re: grandpa—but I've always wanted a tea that smells like fresh chewing tobacco.

WT: You son a bitch, I'm in.

SM: Heathen Tea: Where the words smoke and the leaves burn.

HS: Oh! Cut! Print!

I wish all the world
were as content
as this
contented cat's purr
for then all the world
would rise up!
then, lie down
and
purr purr purr purr purr

"Revolutions never begin comfortably," he said.

```
                              scan\\set
                         ±contextualize°
                            run\/loop
                             >identify
                             >extract
                             >interpret
                         logic//apply
                             >subsume
                         if|then = esc
                             .^resume
                               ~//∞
                             | pilot |



                             *¬query!
                             qudo swot
                             ¶__"frag"
                             gen\\rnd
                         if|then = view
                               /
                               \
          √fragment:/20210813.1120_>>
                               /
                               \
                             load//data
                             scan\\set
                         ±contextualize°
                            run\/loop
                             >identify
                             >extract
                             >interpret
                         logic//apply
                             >subsume
                         if|then = esc
                             .^resume
                               ~//∞
                             | pilot |



                             *¬query!
                         qudo assemble
                             ¶__"expe"
                             gen\\rnd
```

where do we go
when the dreams peel
and the days quake
when the brakes squeal
and the eyes glaze
when the bottles empty
and the hungers gnaw
when the memories bruise
and the limping desire
to connect
    —ejects
like a scratched CD
refusing to play
and the import of who
 and what
  and why
   and how
tick away
with each second
of the clock
you've been staring
 at
for five hours
knowing someday
you will storm this gulf
but today
it swallows you
    —whole

```
01101110 01100001 00100000
01010010 01100101 01100100
01110101 01100011 01110100
01101001 01101111 01101110

01010100 01101000 01100101
00100000 01001101 01101111
01101110 01101011 01100101
01111001 00101101 01000010
01100001 01101110 01100001

01101110 01100001 00100000
01010010 01100101 01100100
01110101 01100011 01110100
01101001 01101111 01101110

01010100 01101000 01100101
00100000 01001101 01101111
01101110 01101011 01100101
1001 00101101 01000010
01101111 01100001
01100001 00100000
100101 01100100
0011 01110100
11 01101110

01100101
101111
0101
010
```

THE MONKEY-BANANA REDUCTION

It happened like this:

I found myself selling a DVD I had never watched, never pulled off the shelf, never removed the shrinkwrap — as new as the day I bought it — and who the, what the hell.

Abruptly I am illumined, as if by spotlight, aware of participating in some weird occulted consumer-materialist ritual, I am stomp-dancing around a jungle campfire, I am *cog in machina*.

Cut to a wide exterior: *cog in machina* smashes through a wall, howl-roars his aliveness, his freedom to rage — then the whispery words of Hovegaard fill the air: "...those. mother. fuckers."

Those motherfuckers, indeed, for what black magic is this, that I paid $19.95 plus tax to temporarily store a brand new, still shrinkwrapped DVD for a decade, then was paid $4.75 via online auction to ship it to Tom in Tulsa?

Do you know how many times I boxed and moved that DVD, and across how many states?

And I still haven't seen that film.

I am certain of this: there is a stick, yet I hold neither the long or the short end. I am only aware there is a schtick: "...*ego sum cog in machina*."

Or, maybe, more rightly:

Ego simia in musa machina.

I am a monkey in the banana machine.

Monkeys and bananas, that's what I reduce the world to.

Fractals.

Repeating patterns.

If everything in the binary world can be reduced to a zero or a one, then fractal-up: to what can we reduce everything in this reality, this now?

I am a _____ and that is a _____.

I am a zero and that is a one.

I am a monkey and that is a banana.

Monkeys and bananas.

Everything is monkeys and bananas.

Behold: THE MONKEY-BANANA REDUCTION.

I am a monkey and when I wake up in the morning I roll out of banana and take a banana, then read the banana while sipping a banana before leaving my banana to drive my banana to (capital B) Banana to earn bananas to buy bananas to wear bananas to eat bananas — and if I don't go to (capital B) Banana to earn bananas, then the monkeys will come and seize my banana, the bananas, and all the bananas.

The level of banana saturation currently being experienced whip-yanks the catheter straight out the banana of any perceived import, the **Good Nurse of Absurdity** grabbing hold and walking away and "*shoo lawd*" you feel it *deep*.

"Oh, God, I wrecked my banana and my banana paid bananas for the banana, but now I owe bananas to monkeys and how am I going to get bananas?!"

"Yeah, I'd like to get a banana on my banana, topped with banana and bananas, and a side of banana."

"Tell you what, I'll give you five bananas for two bananas."

"*Bananas! Get your bananas here!*"

"That monkey just stole my bananas out of my banana!"

"Sir, my monkey is having a monkey, and we need bananas to get bananas for the bananas."

"Yo! My banana's got a banana-*banana* with a *banana*-banana and it's **bananas**."

Do you think there is addiction in the binary world?

Are zeros and ones throwing back shots and slapping down bets on the next number?

Maybe it'll be zero.

Maybe one.

Yes, more Scotch.

No less, Scotch.

Shot. Number. Win.

Shot. Number. Lose.

Shot. One. Lose.

Scotch. Zero. Win.

Shot. Monkey. Win.

1. Zero. 1.

Banana. 0. Lose.

Monkey. Banana. Win.

Banana. Monkey. Banana.

Come mister tally *monkey*, **tally me banana**.

Will you be the Hundredth Monkey?

Perhaps you're the Hundredth Monkey living unawares?

There is the idea, this notion tralala-ing on the fringes of science, popularized by a guy named Watson, that a new idea or behavior will spread near instantaneously from one monkey to all monkeys everywhere once the one-hundredth monkey learns the new idea or behavior. It's like leveling up from binary to quantum: the first one hundred monkeys require direct programming — then all monkeys *just know*.

Boom, done.

This phenomenon was observed in Japanese monkeys on an island in the 1950s using ~~sweet potatoes~~ bananas. The primatologists left bananas for the monkeys and one clever monkey realized it could rinse grit and sand from the banana in some nearby water.

That clever monkey showed another monkey the slick trick, and so it went, monkey by monkey, until Monkey Ninety-Nine showed Monkey One-Hundred and then all the monkeys on the island suddenly *just knew* they could rinse grit and sand from bananas in nearby water, like a patch code spontaneously generated as an over-the-air download and auto-install upgrade for the Monkey Operating System in real-time.

2032 DISHWASHER SALES PROJECTED AT $17B

If Orwell wrote the Hundredth Monkey it would be the **Monkey Ladder Experiment** — a hundred monkeys are placed in a room where at the center is a ladder with bananas at the top. Monkeys being monkeys think *Bananas!* only to be doused with ice cold water upon approach; so it doesn't take long for monkey-math to equate *Bananas!* with HaaHooHee! and suddenly monkey-on-monkey violence is upon them. "If any monkey dare broach *Bananas!* — then, brothers — *cut. him. down.*" bananaically-elected Monkey is heard orating.

And peace and order is restored to the room where at the center stands a ladder with bananas at the top.

And then the experimenters take one monkey out and bring one monkey in and the whole cycle repeats as this new monkey being a monkey thinks *Bananas!* — except this time there is no ice cold water, only bloody bruises and twice-a-week therapy sessions à la the guerrilla assault just delivered by the now-organized monkeys for even thinking *Bananas!*

And so it goes — one out, one in — until the last monkey that knows *Bananas!* means HaaHooHee! is replaced by a monkey who knows *Bananas!* means HeeHaaHoo! and now no monkey *actually* knows why they're not supposed to think *Bananas!*

"Well, *because!*"

From where the monkey stood it was just possible to read the three slogans of the Monkey:

BANANAS! is NO−BANANA
NO−BANANAS! is BANANA
BANANA is BANANAS!

Chancing one further calculation, we arrive at the Infinite Monkey Theorem, which surmises, given infinity, any monkey randomly tap-tapping away at a typewriter will eventually produce the complete works of William Shakespeare.

There is a simple, straightforward proof of this theorem utilizing **THE MONKEY−BANANA REDUCTION**: Willy was a monkey who needed bananas so he produced the complete bananas of Monkey.

The irony here being that there are no bananas in the complete works of William Shakespeare.

15 apples, eight figs, and one lemon, but no bananas.

Willy was a monkey who never wrote the word **banana**.

This is known as the Shakespeare Exception — or the Shakeception — to **THE MONKEY-BANANA REDUCTION** because there's always *that one monkey* . . .

This is my banana.

There are many like it but this one's mine.

My banana is my best friend.

It is my banana.

I must master it as I must master me, Monkey.

Without me, my banana is useless.

Without my banana, I am useless.

I must fire my banana true.

I must banana straighter than my enemy who is trying to banana me.

I must banana him before he bananas me.

I will!

Before Monkey, I swear this creed:

My banana and me, Monkey, are defenders of my banana.

We are the bananas of our monkey.

We are the monkeys of my banana.

So be it, until there is no monkey, but banana.

Banana!

Then the face of the monkey faded away again, and instead the three slogans of the Monkey stood out in bold capitals:

BANANAS! is **NO−BANANA**

NO−BANANAS! is **BANANA**

BANANA is **BANANAS!**

It has been said that "the shit" *is* bananas.

Utilizing **THE MONKEY-BANANA REDUCTION**, I agree.

B – A – N – A – N – A – S.

Does that monkey Bigfoot like bananas?

What about that monkey Ted Cruz? Tom Cruise?

I had a friend once, he was — after I had just explained **THE MONKEY-BANANA REDUCTION** to him — raving about this dish he enjoyed at a Jamaican restaurant.

"Dude, it was so good, I need it again right now."

"What was it?"

"I don't know! But dude, so good — I wonder if they have an online menu? Hold on . . . "

His face fell, "Plantains."

"What?"

"The dish, it was plantains."

"Oh, yeah, monkey?!"

> plantain, *n.*   tree-like tropical herbaceous plant allied to banana and bearing similar fruit; its fruit.

Somewhere monkeys are jumping out of bananas.

Somewhere monkeys are growing bananas in petri dishes.

Somewhere **cog in machina** roar-howls.

Somewhere a monkey plots your banana . . .

ROMEO
Your plantain-leaf is excellent for that.

Romeo and Juliet: Act 1, Scene 2, Line 51

"That monkey bananaed that monkey over bananas!"

"He just—he just lost all his bananas and went *bananas*."

It was the best of bananas, it was the worst of bananas . . .

"An organized and highly sophisticated group of monkeys executed the daring heist of Priceless Banana at the Metropolitan Banana of Modern Banana today — a monkey could be heard saying, 'Come mister tally monkey, tally me banana.'"

> *A beautiful bunch of ripe banana*
> *(Daylight come and me wanna go home)*
> *Hide the deadly black tarantula*
> *(Daylight come and me wanna go home)*

Ever seen The Monkees movie **Head**?

I haven't because I never took it off the shelf.

That's maybe the most absurd part, there was more than one brand new, still shinkwrapped DVD.

Repetition was necessary to learn this cosmic lesson — it wasn't enough that there was one —— *there were many Toms in Tulsa.*

Over the course of 17 years, I amassed over one thousand films in various formats.

Once shelved, it was a wall of movies.

An entire wall.

A monument.

A (capital W) Wall of bananas.

One which made me feel accomplished(.)

> *as jungle drums echo in the distance.*
> *as a monkey cowers in awe of the monolith.*

I can remember the first DVD I purchased was Ridley Scott's *Gladiator* starring Russell Crowe(.)

> *as the perennial primal vein pulses.*

It was 2000 and I had just moved into my first apartment. I don't remember purchasing the DVD player, but I do remember purchasing *Gladiator*.

"Are you not entertained?!"

> *as I stomp-dance around a jungle campfire.*

At some point, much later, I convinced myself that the wall of movies was my diploma.

Some filmmakers have certificates from USC or NYU framed on their wall.

I had an *entire wall* of movies.

Each DVD, each Blu-ray, a credit and further proof that I had "earned" the right to call myself filmmaker.

`Do not be fooled` — this entitlement was fueled by the delusion of self education via unmitigated consumerist materialism — where box sets are extra credits, foreign films are electives, and **CRITERION** means AP — and I was acing the class.

This thought process makes *perfect sense* to one borne of a lower middle class Appalachian upbringing where *stuff = success*.

"I am not a number, I am a free monkey!"

Somewhere along the way, if you're not careful, the words "student" and "hoarder" blur together . . .

Evidence of this shift manifests easily enough, why else would at least a quarter of the films *in the wall* still bear their shrinkwrap?

Movies shelved with shrinkwrap intact is unbecoming of a proper cinéaste.

If you truly love (capital F) Film, then you commit to the immediate 90% loss in value by ripping the shrinkwrap from the case and submitting to its contents as soon as possible.

Preferably more than once.

A lot would be nice.

If it's Kevin Smith's **MALLRATS** (the theatrical cut, which is the better cut, I'll fight you on this), then memorizing the entire film and reciting each line while anyone dares watch with you is irrefragably required.

File Troy Duffy's **The Boondock Saints** in that folder, too. Commitment.

Two can be as bad as one

And that was my second realization: that I rarely watch movies more than once.

It's not that I won't, it's just that I generally don't.

I used to, but at some point in my late 20s, when the option became watch **Raiders of the Lost Ark** for the umphundredth time or watch *A Woman Under the Influence* for the first time, that's when the unknown-to-me films began to consistently win my attention (and how Cassavetes became my favorite) with the dawning realization of just how many unknown-to-me films were still out there growing exponentially.

Come mister tally monkey, tally me banana.

Watch six film, seven film, eight film bunch (Daylight come and me wanna go home)

Ever seen The Monkees movie *Head*?

I just watched it.

My mother says that old men always say they're "gonna" — "I'm *gonna* do this, I'm *gonna* do that, but they never do."

In old man parlance *gonna* = *not doing*.

And *not doing* means not at this very moment, no, and also in the future likely never, too.

I said likely.

Potential is a spectrum.

When my home phone detects an incoming robocall, it announces it as "Potential Spam."

Do you think Potential Spam is the Beyond Meat of the Spamverse?

And so "I'm *gonna* watch *Head.*"

Became "I'm watching *Head.*"

Became "I watched *Head.*"

I think the film is a fantastic exploration of the importance of understanding group dynamics while tripping on psychedelics with two or more persons — for once we are on the journey it is not until we all return to the bridge of understanding that we can truly plunge into the depths of the experience together.

In stoner speak: *get on my level.*

~~He was another one in a sea of zeros.~~

Jack Nicholson for sure tripped psychedelics. You can see it in his writing: *Ride in the Whirlwind*, **The Trip**, *Head*. In all you see Nicholson fiddling with linear time, looping it, inverting it so that, hold on, we've been here before, haven't we? — wait a sec

~~— another zero in a sea of ones.~~

But we can't hold on can't wait because time must be experienced moving forward be damned linearity because time cannot can not,

~~Join the One Army today!~~

We're one but we're not the same

(Daylight come and me wanna go home)

Ever seen The Monkees movie *Head*?

Utilizing **THE MONKEY-BANANA REDUCTION** all bands become The Monkeys.

The Rolling Stones become The Monkeys.

The Smiths become The Monkeys.

The Beatles become The Monkeys.

The Arctic Monkeys become The Monkeys.

The Monkees become The Monkeys.

I imagine Sisyphus pushing, grunting, humming:

Oh, how many times do I have to make this climb?

I imagine Prometheus eyeing the eagle at dawn:

Do I have to do this all over again?

Oasis becomes Monkey.

Queen becomes Monkey.

ㆍ↕ ⇦⇨⇦↕↘⇨▽ ℧⇊

If The Beatles become The Monkees, then her ticket to ride will be on the last train to

COME IN, DO YOU READ?

The Eagles become

come in, hello hello

—Floyd becomes Mon—

. . . ANYBODY OUT THERE?

Fatboy Slim becomes Monman Key. (Probably.)

Do you think as time collapses in on itself, that the myths of Sisyphus and Prometheus will coalesce into the monomyth of Sisymetheus, the god who stole fire from the gods and gifted it to humans and, for his crime, was sentenced to eternity rolling a boulder up hill (again) while an eagle pecked out his liver (again)?

Beck becomes Monkey, but he knows.

I felt it, just now, the ripple, the disturbance, some *one* already thought that was the myth — *it has begun* . . .

In the time of chimpanzees I was a monkey

Gorillaz become Monkeyz.

Don't banana, get it, get it

The **Marshmallow Test** becomes the **Banana Test** when reduced.

A person sits one banana in front of you and says, "I am going to set this one banana, here, in front of you and I am going to go away for fifteen minutes and when I come back, if this one banana is still here, in front of you, then I will give you a second banana."

And so that person leaves and your test of Reasoning, Discipline, and Give-a-Shit begins.

- **Reasoning** first because do you want two bananas?
  — If no, eat one banana now.
  — If yes, see Discipline.
- **Discipline** second because how badly do you want two bananas?
  — If no, eat one banana now.
  — If yes, see Give-a-Shit.
- **Give-a-Shit** third because:
  — If no, eat one banana now.
  — If yes, then the burden of who you *actually* are as a monkey comes to bear full weight because to achieve second banana can you truly wait fifteen minutes; sixty minutes; a thousand minutes . . .

Once in a lifetime?

Like a leaden banana the words came back at him:

BANANAS! is NO-BANANA
NO-BANANAS! is BANANA
BANANA is BANANAS!

```
01010101 01101110 01100100 01100101 01110010
01110111 01101111 01110010 01101100 01100100
00100000 01100010 01100101 01100011 01101111
01101101 01100101 01110011 00100000 01001101
01101111 01101110 01101011 01100101 01111001
```

I don't mean to be the thing you don't want me to be

A squat yellow banana of only thirty-four bananas. Over the main banana the words, Central London Bananaery and Bananaing Centre, and, in a shield, the Banana's motto, BANANA, BANANAS, BANANA.

Repeat: Monkey has taken Banana

— and monkey only then becomes Monkey in the complete sense of the word, when his punctuation includes no question marks, only exclamation points, commas, and periods —

and bananas.

"And this," said the Monkey opening the door, "is the Banana Room."

It is a truth universally acknowledged, that a single monkey in possession of a good banana, must be in want of a monkey.

"Oh, Monkey," Monkey said, "we could have had such a damned good banana together."

Ahead was a mounted monkey in khaki directing traffic. He raised his banana. The banana slowed suddenly pressing Monkey against me.

"Yes," I said. "Isn't it bananas to think so?"

REPEAT: MONKEY HAS BANANA

And so I sold them: the DVDs, the Blu-rays, all the bananas.

Gifted the epiphany that I, (capital M) Monkey, had with a (capital W) Wall of bananas been supplanting a wall-hanging (capital D) Diploma as proof I had "earned" the title of (capital F) Filmmaker freed me from the burden of sustaining the (capital W) Wall of bananas.

An entire wall.

A monument.

And so it fell like the (capital W) Wall of Berlin I had watched on television in my youth, monkeys with bananas chipping away at Banana, freeing bananas to their monkeys, Toms in Tulsa all.

The banana-wielding monkey shatters the monolith.

And then I started _____ing bananas and now I have four Walls of bananas.

REPEAT: MONKEY – BANANA, OVER

The long-hoped-for banana was entering his banana.

He gazed up at the enormous banana.

Forty years it had taken him to learn what kind of banana was hidden beneath the dark banana.

O cruel, needless misbananaing!

O stubborn, self-willed exile from the loving banana!

Two banana-scented tears trickled down the sides of his banana.

But it was all right, everything was all right, the struggle was finished.

He had won the victory over monkey.

He loved Banana.

Ba-na-na-na-nah
It's the 'nana lovin' Mon-K-double-E (MonKee!)
Ba-na-na-na-nah

For Banana must win.

Stack banana till the morning come
(Daylight come and me wanna go home)

I am banana.

"I, Banana."

Ba-na-na-na-nah

Somewhere **cog in machina** howls.

One day the ebb will flow
and a wave of fortunes untold
will crash upon my shore . . .
until then, I can only emulate
that which the tide does: *persist*.

scan\\set
±contextualize°
run\/loop
>identify
>extract
>interpret
logic//apply
>subsume
if|then = esc
.resume
~//∞
| piLot |

*>query!
qudo swot
¶__"frag"
gen\\rnd
if|then = view
/
\

fragment:/20160921.0053_>>

/
\
.load//data
scan\\set
±contextualize°
run\/loop
>identify
>extract
>interpret
logic//apply
>subsume
if|then = esc
.resume
~//∞
| piLot |

*>query!
qudo assemble
¶__"expe"
gen\\rnd

I will return to it.
Love rewrote I-code at root level, then rebooted.
On the way, everything remembered, I became You.
You like before, except better because—
You danced a cosmic dance, danced for eons.
Two tabs took you there, to the Infinite Plane.
On the way, everything forgotten, You became I.
I corresponded with Love: >>The Brilliant White Light<<
In Love's presence, I knew:
- I was a part of it.
- I was apart from it.
- I will return to it.
Love rewrote I-code at root level, then rebooted.
On the way, everything remembered, I became You.
You like before, except better because—

You danced a cosmic dance, danced for eons.
Two tabs took you there, to the Infinite Plane.
On the way, everything forgotten, You became I.
I corresponded with Love: >>The Brilliant White Light<<
In Love's presence, I knew:

- I was a part of it.
- I was apart from it.
- I will return to it.

Love rewrote I-code at root level, then rebooted.
On the way, everything remembered, I became You.
You like before, except better because—
You danced a cosmic dance, danced for eons.

Two tabs took you there, to the Infinite Plane.
On the way, everything forgotten, You became I.
I corresponded with Love: >>The Brilliant White Light<<
In Love's presence, I knew:
- I was a part of it.
- I was apart from it.
- I will return to it.
Love rewrote I-code at root level, then rebooted.
On the way, everything remembered, I became You.
You like before, except better because—
You danced a cosmic dance, danced for eons.
Two tabs took you there, to the Infinite Plane.
On the way, everything forgotten, You became I.
I corresponded with Love: >>The Brilliant White Light<<
In Love's presence, I knew:
- I was a part of it.

AN
INCONSEQUENTIAL
EXPLOIT
OF
KAPITäN SCHADENFREUDE

"The Lumen Frame"

de la mente de
Sheboygan Minnetonka

schadenfreude
noun

A German word that translates literally as "harm-joy"
used to express delight in another's misfortune

BLACK.

Pre-lap: Room tone, then--

**INT. WHAT MIGHT BE CALLED A STAGE - DAY
(16:9 ASPECT RATIO)**

A poorly-lit makeshift theater curtain.

KING JAMES sidesteps into view, frame left.

Hair slicked down, helmet-like, he wears
a tuxedo T-shirt, a monocle, and something
that looks like a mustache.

He clears his throat, then again, then--

> KING JAMES
> Welcome, extinguished guests.
> (gestures at curtain)
> Beyond this veil your destiny lies
> in wait -- awaiting -- for ye are
> soon to symbiose with inappreciable
> syncopations beyond your wildest
> imaginations and most truly
> scrumptious envisagations, a tale
> whose tell is a title never told,
> but in this telling the told tale
> is titled...
> (clumsily grandiose)
> An Inconsequential Exploit of
> *Kapitän Schadenfreude.*

AN ARM, from off camera, hurtles into frame
and bare-knuckle punches King James square in
his right deltoid causing the monocle to leap
from his eye...

King James fully experiences the pain, then
leers at the The-One-Who-Punched off camera--

> KING JAMES
> (sotto)
> *son-of-uh-bean-dip, motherfritos!*
> (beat)
> That really hurt.

King James pulls up his shirt sleeve, surveys the damage...

> KING JAMES
> I'm bruised?

He fires a shocked look at The-One-Who-Punched--

> KING JAMES
> You flippin' bruised me! Do you see that? Do you see that, pal, that motherflippin' bruise right there?!

> SIR NICK (O.S.)
> (quoting *Star Wars*)
> "Stay on target."

King James whips around in SIR NICK's direction, his fake mustache catches up--

> KING JAMES
> I have been physically assaulted!

> SIR NICK (O.S.)
> (quoting *Star Wars*)
> *"Stay on target!"*

A tsunami of disgust swallows King James as he cradles his deltoid, looks beyond camera and around the set, searching faces--

> KING JAMES
> And we're okay with this? Everyone's all okay? We're all good? This is good? This is fine? We're fine?

He looks directly into camera, still babying the deltoid--

> KING JAMES
> You're okay with this?
> (beat)
> You sure?

His gaze drifts from camera, processing,

accepting his fate--

>   KING JAMES
>   (quoting Shakespeare)
>   "...though I go alone, Like to a
>   lonely dragon..."

A DIFFERENT ANGLE

Everyone, including crew, perform a back-to-one reset as King James returns the monocle to his eye and readies himself.

Then, as if nothing happened--

>   KING JAMES
>   Inconsequential because it does not
>   matter. Exploitive in all the ways
>   that do.
>   (German accent)
>   *Kapitän* because he is *zee German!*

James performs a German military heel click.

>   KING JAMES
>   And *Schadenfreude* because...
>   (yep)
>   (that's right)
>   ...you.

He gestures at the curtain as it inelegantly parts and we dolly-in to reveal--

INT. ROOM - DAY (4:3 ASPECT RATIO)

We hear a clock ticking, *60 Minutes*-style: tk-tk-tk-tk-tk

Note: It never stops tk-tk-tk-tk-ticking.

Also note: This is a wildly kinetic live-action anime moving at double-time; you should be reading so fast you're out of breath starting now:

KAPITÄN SCHADENFREUDE enters, reaches, flips a light switch. His uniform is somewhere

between trick-or-treat chic and Hotels.com
Captain Obvious.

The bulb briefly illumines, then BZT-POP!
dies--

VHS TITLE SCREEN:

> AN INCONSEQUENTIAL EXPLOIT OF
> KAPITÄN SCHADENFREUDE
>
> "THE LUMEN FRAME"

INT. ROOM - CONTINUOUS

Kapitän Schadenfreude stares at the blown
bulb: tk-tk-tk-tk

> KAPITÄN SCHADENFREUDE
> (anime-style)
> *Ehh-mhm...*

He surveys the room, notices a stool--

CLOSER

An anime-style light gleam ensures we notice
the stool.

WIDER

Kapitän again surveys the room, notices a
package of brand-new, overtly-staged light
bulbs nearby.

> KAPITÄN SCHADENFREUDE
> (anime-style)
> *Eh-mm?*

CLOSER

An anime-style light gleam ensures we notice
the new bulbs.

WIDER

Kapitän looks from the brand-new bulbs to the
stool to the blown bulb, puts it all together

as they gleam in unison--

> KAPITÄN SCHADENFREUDE
> (Japanese)
>> *Mmm. Hai!*

RAPID-FIRE SHOTS:

- Kapitän grabs the new bulbs.

- Kapitän grabs the stool.

- Kapitän rips open the package of new bulbs.

- Kapitän positions the stool.

- Kapitän extracts a brand-new bulb, it sparkles.

- Kapitän steps up onto the stool, then--

THE BLOWN BULB

Appears top center frame, tk-tk-tk-tk-tk... as Kapitän's stretching, struggling fingers slooooowly enter bottom center frame... inching closer, then closer to the bulb--

THE STOOL

Appears wobbly and unsteady as Kapitän slowly rises to his tippy-toes while trying to maintain balance...

KAPITÄN'S FACE

Appears distorted and anime-style red as sweat breaks out on his forehead, his eyes locked on the bulb.

> KAPITÄN SCHADENFREUDE
> (anime-style)
>> *Ehh-rr-uh...*

THE BLOWN BULB

As Kapitän's fingers finally touch the bulb and he tries, then tries again to unscrew it... *it will not move...*

KAPITÄN'S FACE

As he scowls, refocuses his attention, really commits--

THE BLOWN BULB

As he again tries to unscrew it and -- ERR-RKT -- it moves!

KAPITÄN'S FACE

As the scowl becomes a smile; suddenly his eyes dart left--

KAPITÄN POV

As we dutch-angle crash-zoom into empty space--

KAPITÄN'S FACE

As his eyes go wide and dart right--

KAPITÄN POV

As we dolly zoom into nothing--

KAPITÄN'S FACE

As his eyes roll, then dart upward--

KAPITÄN POV

As the picture begins rotating, separating into red, green, and blue channels--

KAPITÄN'S FACE

As he blinks, tries to shake it off, eyes dart downward--

KAPITÄN POV

King James sits in profile screaming monkey noises at a bottle of mayonnaise he's holding above his head as he squeezes it forcing an

unending stream of mayo all over his face
while he furiously masturbates a very real
still-in-its-peel banana lubed to excess with
mayo sticking out of his pants.

However, the shot blinks by so quickly we
really can't be sure of any of that.

KAPITÄN'S FACE

Appears anime-style green as he throws up a
little in his mouth; he tries to shake off
the image, but then--

KAPITÄN POV

King James is now surrounded by SEVEN PEOPLE
IN MONKEY MASKS, all screaming monkey noises
as they masturbate their own mayo-slathered
bananas.

Behind them, squatting on a stool, is SOMEONE
IN A MONKEY MASK, not participating in the
monkerwauling circle jerk, but eating their
banana because--

FREEZE FRAME - MOS (SFX: BELL DING!)

An arrow points at the banana-eating monkey.

SUPER: There's always *that one monkey*...

KAPITÄN'S FACE

As his eyes go wide, terrified, then we
parallax to reveal, over Kapitän's shoulder,
THE BIG O standing in the doorway.

> THE BIG O
> Hey, what's happ*inän*', *Kapitän*?

WIDER

Kapitän exits his delirium--

> KAPITÄN SCHADENFREUDE
> (anime-style)
> *Erh-hmm?*

8.

He turns to face The Big O. tk-tk-tk-tk-tk

EXTREME WIDE

Kapitän looks from The Big O to the brand-new
bulb in his hand to the stool he's standing
on to the blown bulb, puts it all together as
they gleam in unison (including The Big O)--

> KAPITÄN SCHADENFREUDE
> (Japanese)
> *Mmm. Hai!*

RAPID-FIRE SHOTS:

- Kapitän grabs The Big O by the arm, yanks
them out of frame.

- Kapitän pushes The Big O up onto the stool.

> THE BIG O
> No, really, what is happening?

- Kapitän hands The Big O the new bulb.

- Kapitän wildly gesticulates at the blown
bulb.

- Kapitän flips the switch on-off-on-off-on-
off-on-off--

WIDER

Kapitän returns to The Big O, points at the
bulb, and screams--

Note: There was an error in the English
subtitle programming for this episode, but
they are required by corporate, so...

KAPITÄN SCHADENFREUDE	ENGLISH SUBTITLE
(approximate Russian)	Hey, y'all, today we're
A demon hellspawn has	gonna be baking my
vanquished the glow-globe	favorite: grandma's
and now it must rebirth!	fudgy chocolate chip
	cookies.

Beat.

>   THE BIG O
>   The bulb needs replaced?

Kapitän blinks, uncomprehending.

The Big O mimes replacing the bulb.

>   KAPITÄN SCHADENFREUDE
>   (Japanese)
>   *Mm. Hai!*

>   THE BIG O
>   Okay... I guess I'll just...
>   ...replace the bulb, then?
>   (quoting Mario)
>   ...*Here we go!*

THE BLOWN BULB

Appears top center frame, tk-tk-tk-tk-tk...
as The Big O's stretching, struggling fingers
slooooowly enter bottom center frame...
inching closer, then closer to the bulb, as--

KAPITÄN SCHADENFREUDE	ENGLISH SUBTITLE
(approximate Russian)	In a large bowl, cream
Do you know why you will	together the butter and
fail in this task?! It	sugar until they are
is because you are a	velvety smooth.
failure!	

THE STOOL

Appears wobbly and unsteady as The Big O
slowly rises to their tippy-toes while trying
to maintain balance...

KAPITÄN SCHADENFREUDE	ENGLISH SUBTITLE
(approximate Russian)	Now, if you want that
You are a worthless	fudgier texture and
nothing whose long list	the softest gosh-durn
of failures...	cookies...

THE BIG O'S FACE

Appears distorted and anime-style red as

10.

sweat breaks out on their forehead, their
eyes locked on the bulb.

KAPITÄN SCHADENFREUDE	ENGLISH SUBTITLE
(approximate Russian)	...this side of the
...is as long as the	Mississippi, be sure
Mississippi! You will	your butter is at room
never succeed because you	temperature. mmmm-mmm-
are a fail-huh-URE!	MMM!

WIDER

The Big O stops, looks at Kapitän--

> THE BIG O
> ...is that really necessary?

> KAPITÄN SCHADENFREUDE
> (Japanese)
> *Mm. Hai!*

> THE BIG O
> No. Not Hai. *No Hai!* Please stop.

The Big O again reaches for--

THE BLOWN BULB

As their fingers finally touch the bulb and
they try, then try again to unscrew it, when
-- ERR-RKT -- it moves!

KAPITÄN SCHADENFREUDE	ENGLISH SUBTITLE
(approximate Russian)	Beat in the vanilla and
I will soon delight in	eggs one at a time,
this very next stupendous	then combine the flour,
blunder of yours! It will	baking soda, and salt
be such a grandly epic	and stir it all into the
feast of failure!	sugar mixture.

The bulb is really ERK-ERK-ERK moving now,
almost there...

WIDER

The Big O begins to relax as the bulb is

almost out--

KAPITÄN SCHADENFREUDE
(approximate Russian)
The time of your greatest
fault has risen! I
cannot wait to bake in
the magnificent glory of
this, your most delicious
fiasco!

ENGLISH SUBTITLE
Then, mix in your
chocolate chips, and
dollop tablespoonfuls
onto an ungreased cookie
sheet. Next, bake them
for about ten minutes in
a preheated oven.

CLOSER

As the receptacle finally releases its grasp
on the bulb, but to the surprise of The
Big O, who drops, saves, fumbles, catches,
fumbles, then drops both bulbs--

THE BLOWN BULB

Hits the floor and shatters.

THE BRAND-NEW BULB

Hits the floor and shatters.

EXTREME WIDE

tk-tk-tk-tk-tk

The Big O slouches in defeat.

tk-tk-tk-tk-tk

Kapitän inhales deeply and laughs a big
anime-style belly laugh.

ANGLE ON

Kapitän as he slaps The Big O on the back--

KAPITÄN SCHADENFREUDE
(Japanese accent)
Kapitän Schadenfreude has-uh...
STRUCK AGAIN!

The Big O might cry.

He laughs bigger, then bigger, then--

12.

VHS TITLE SCREEN:

THE FOLLOWING HAS BEEN
A MEDITATION ON SOCIAL MEDIA
AND YOU WHO ENGAGE IT

ROLL CREDITS
WITH MUZAK

POST-CREDITS TAG

Where we left them, Kapitän laughing even
bigger...

tk-tk-tk-tk-tk

THE BIG O
I don't know why, but I need some
chocolate chip cookies... like,
right now.

and every bridge
I ever burnt
I burnt the same:

            in a holocaust
                of nuclear flame

```
                                    scan\\set
                              ±contextualize°
                                 run\/loop
                                  >identify
                                  >extract
                                  >interpret
                              logic//apply
                                  >subsume
                              if|then = esc
                                  .^resume
                                    ~//∞
                                  | piLot |


                                  *¬query!
                              qudo swot
                              ¶__"frag"
                              gen\\rnd
                          if|then = view
                                    /
                                    \
        √fragment://20250210.1223_>>
                                    /
                                    \
                              load//data
                              scan\\set
                              ±contextualize°
                                 run\/loop
                                  >identify
                                  >extract
                                  >interpret
                              logic//apply
                                  >subsume
                              if|then = esc
                                  .^resume
                                    ~//∞
                                  | piLot |


                                  *¬query!
                              qudo assemble
                              ¶__"expe"
                              gen\\rnd
```

is this how we implode?

like a bullet shot at 800,000 fps
  resolving toward a violent predestination
  slowly, then slower...
  splintering shattered hearts
  inverting dime-store egos
  cosmic, ethereal grandeur in the dissolution

give ear: haunting, recurring echoes...

    corrupt promises = no restitution

    intrinsically perverted = each justification

    spiritual abrasion ≥ post-traumatic

    automatic teaming axiomatic

disappointment, this:
  what it means to be human
  the bullet, collapsing upon itself
  slowly, yet slower...
  laboring recognition
  lo! asseveration:

      — we have arrived
      — we never arrived

is this how we implode?

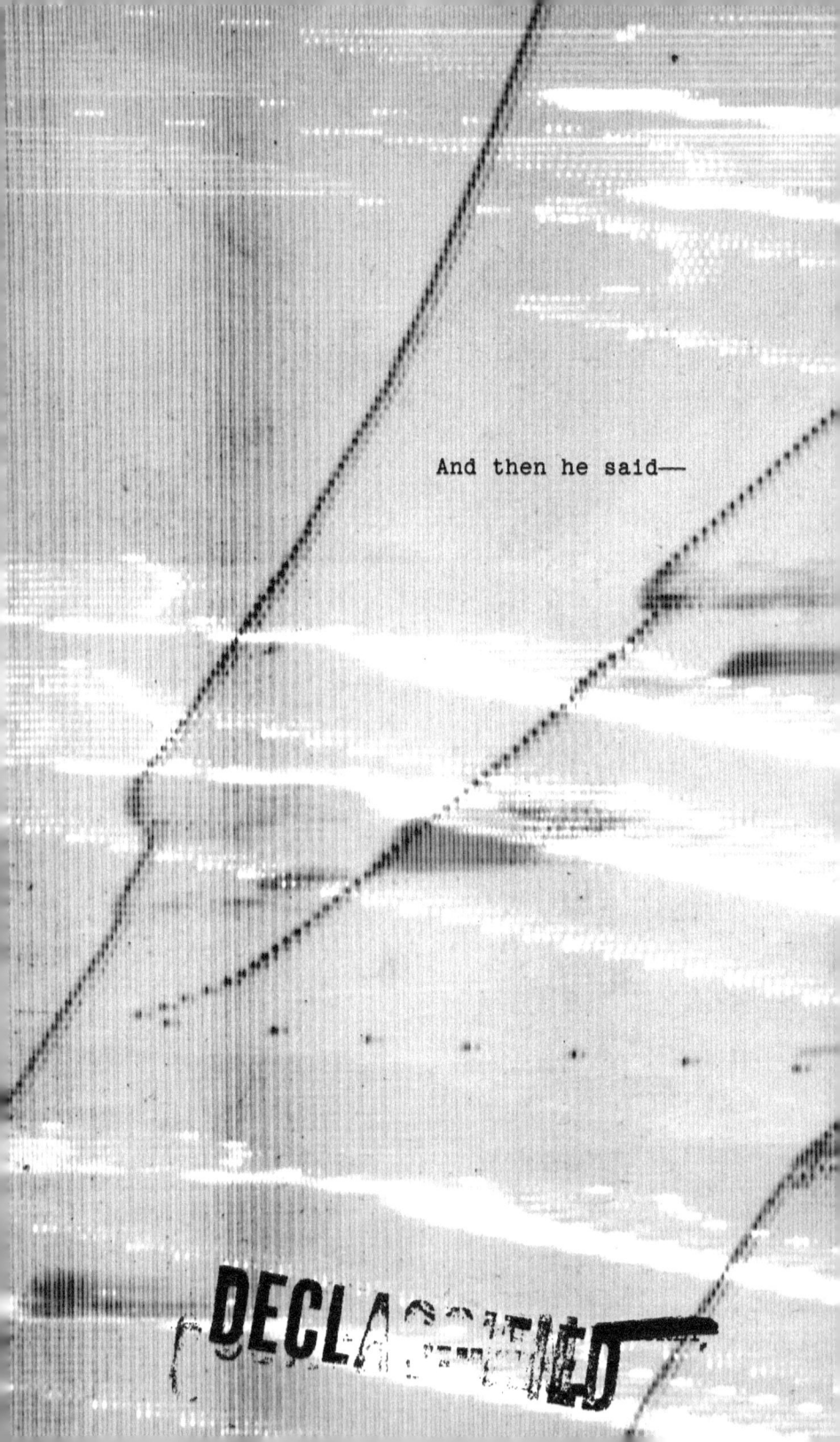

And then he said—

DECLASSIFIED

DECLASSIFIED

"You rock like a Bach opera."

A Conversation with Cassavetes.[1]

The true significance of why I have a giant Cassavetes poster haphazardly hanging above my desk had, so far, eluded me. I knew I liked the image. I knew I liked the director. And I knew there was something deeper that I just couldn't quite — *mphh*.

You know?

Like, there's this vein that Cassavetes tapped that everyone around bought into and it was divine when a shutter clicked twenty-four times in a second. Because they didn't know. But John knew. Like he knows it right now, staring down at me, and looking up at me at the same time. Simultaneously taunting and encouraging me.

"What?"

C'mon, man.

"What."

I don't know, I mean, does it have to be so — on the nose?

"High on three tabs, asking 'on the nose?' Look, right now the answer is love. To all of your problems. Always love. The sooner you get that, the better. Tell your truth, always, because love."

Dude.

"Got it?"

Yes?

---

[1] Imagined while on a three-tab gentle glide, of course.

"No."

Maybe a moment; Ravi Shankar's "Raga Jog" sitar echoing.

Maybe he hits a cigarette, rubs the back of his neck: the beat poet feeling the next wave.

Maybe I should smoke again . . . [2]

"Your parents couldn't figure it out when you were eight and now you sabotage anything that starts going well for you. The nearer your heart, the brighter the flame. And so it goes, or has gone, until we're here now, you and I. Look, you're never gonna get lower than me unless you're in the dirt. You see? I'm literally hugging the earth. And you're never gonna get higher than me sitting at that keyboard. You see? I'm literally hanging above you. But that's right where you need me: halfway between the gutter and the stars, kid. Now, are we going to tell some fucking stories or what?"

I'm typing, man, I'm typing, as fast as my fingers can backspace, I'm typing.

"Good. Keep doing that. Christ, I'm hungry."

Chipotle would be amazing right now. Burrito bowl for here. Brown rice, both beans . . . half chicken, half steak, fajita veggies, two scoops of hot salsa, cheese, guac, lettuce. A regular drink. Approximately ninety percent unsweetened, ten sweet. Wait, I only do that when I get my own tea. I don't think I could look at anyone and ask for those percentages with a straight face.

"The poster, saboteur."

What?

"Tell them about me."

Right now?

"They're called breadcrumbs. This is how we keep stories interesting, with breadcrumbs. Go on."

It's a William Clax—

Wait, I can't just tell the story about the poster unless I tell the *whole story*.

---

[2] Weed, of course.

"See, now we're getting somewhere."

Dude, I literally only came down here to update my iTunes account info so I could purchase this Ravi Shankar album.

Maybe another moment; "Raga Jog" sitar still echoing . . .

"Stop it."

What?

"Trying to be clever."

Breadcrumbs?

"Earn it. You even admitted to yourself three hours ago that when you try to be clever you fail. So don't do that anymore. And you only literally came down here like I'm literally hugging the earth and literally hanging above you. See, everything matters . . . *the bird and the butterfly*."

Breadcrumbs?

"Now you're trying to be clever again and you're struggling. That cursor just waiting, blinking in anticipation: the amateur feeling the next wave."

Hey, that's my line! And, I mean, I won't disagree.

"Humility. That will serve you well."

> humility, *n.*   a modest or low view of one's own importance; humbleness.

"Balanced with ego."

> ego, *n.*   a person's sense of self-esteem or self-importance.

"Deeper."

> ego, *psychoanalysis.*   the part of the mind that mediates between the conscious and the unconscious and is responsible for reality testing and a sense of personal identity.

"Your truth."
Personal identity?
"Yes."
But, blinking cursor.
"Wait it out."
How long?
"The amateur waiting . . . Raga done? Put on some jazz. Real jazz."
Coltrane? Davis? Jarrett? It's all real, right? "Take Five"?
"Brubeck?"
Too whimsical?
"Deeper."
Bitches Brew.
"Turn it up. Let it flow."
Chaos.
"In the best way."
Fuck. Yes.
"Ready?"
Here we go.

It's a jolt.

Always.

No fade up, just hard cut, and there I am: Aunt T's hand in my left, baby bottle in my right, walking down a movie theater aisle at the exact moment when an unseen E.T. throws the baseball back to Elliott and it rolls to a stop at his feet.

For the longest time I was never sure if this memory was real or not, but from all accounts I'm certain this is my first memory of life.

I told a friend that once. Daniel. He said, "Auspicious beginnings."

I had to look it up.

auspicious, *adj.*   giving or being a sign of future success.

At the time I remember thinking that might be a cool part of my story someday.

"But you're not a filmmaker, so who gives a shit."

But that's ten minutes into the film, so I could never quite figure out how all of those elements aligned exactly to form that specific memory, so I asked Aunt T, "Did you take me to see *E.T.* when I was little?"

"Yes. Gosh, you were little!"

"Did we show up late?"

She had to think for a second — *memory retrieved*:

"Yes, actually. I had to work that night and we got to the theater late. How do you remember that?"

"Auspicious beginnings."

"But you're not a filmmaker, so who gives a shit."

"Clever boy."

Too many voices.

I guess this is like meditating, right? You try to maintain the focus until you lose it, become aware that you've lost it, then try to regain it.

"Stop trying to be clever and you won't lose focus."

Write just right and you'll always just write.

Is that like perfect-practice makes perfect?

Breadcrumbs.

"And jazz, baby!"

Oh, God. Nine hundred ninety-nine words. Is this any good? One thousand and eight now. Twenty-six hundred is a good day?

I like the idea of an anti-novel because it's a bit carte blanche.

"Like jazz, baby!"

Maybe that's what I need, some literary jazz?

Maybe *The Great American Novel* was the whop I needed.

I haven't written anything in three years. I've just been in my head the whole time.

I did write a short film. A sci-fi comedy about quantum

modularity and spatial displacement. It's clever, that's why you haven't heard of it.

What's the opposite of a breadcrumb? Like, a reverse breadcrumb?

"That's a callback."

> callback, **n.**   a second or additional audition for a theatrical part.

"Trying for Hamlet?"

Sorry, further down—

> callback, **n.**   a comedic technique that extends a previous joke with a new but related joke.

"I see what you did there."

Breadcrumb or callback?

Maybe both? (Except imagine we said it at the same time.)

"Unearned!"

Really?

Eleven fifty-eight.

Twenty-six seems so far.

I think that's all I have in me.

"You're out?"

Let's not make a thing of it. I'm tired, and this is jazz, baby.

I'll be back—

—will you?

"That sounds like a setup."

> setup, **n.**   the deliberate introduction of a narrative element that primes the audience for a future payoff.

```
                    scan\\
              ±contextualize°
                  run\/loop
                  >identify
                   >extract
                  >interpret
              logic//apply
                  >subsume
              if|then = esc
                  .^resume
                    ~//∞
                  | pilot |



                   *¬query!
                  qudo swot
                  ¶__"frag"
                  gem\\rnd
              if|then = view
                        /
                        \
```

√fragment:/20230808.1727_

```
                        /
                        \
                  load//data
                  scan\\set
              ±contextualize°
                  run\/loop
                  >identify
                   >extract
                  >interpret
              logic//apply
                  >subsume
              if|then = esc
                  .^resume
                    ~//∞
                  | pilot |



                   *¬query!
              qudo assemble
                  ¶__"expe"
                  gen\\rnd
```

```
You put too much faith in me
      _and now you're disappointed.
Goød.
God.
Your faith was {
    #misplaced: A;
}
    _misguided mistake
          _you'll always make.
Because we always fail, always.
It's the cycle, this journey
    _valleys inevitable.
And we've only just met
    _kismet, I suspect
          /* null set roulette */
              _I expect
                  _videlicet:
Aim higher, Trier
    _preciser
          _near nonpareil.
And bless your faith
    _in Faith
          _we won't fail...


Again.
```

Every *thing* is a note,
Every *interaction* a chord,
Every *life* a movement:
The *symphony* of the universe . . .

WADE THOMAS

HONORARY HEATHEN

ACKNOWLEDGMENTS

WATSON THOMAS
would like to thank:
God, psychedelics, the Brilliant White Light,
the Co-Heathens, my cats (past and present),
my chickens (past and present),
John Cassavetes, Steven "Schizopolis" Soderbergh,
and _____.

(You probably think this blank is about you, don't you, don't you…)

SHEBOYGAN MINNETONKA
would like to thank:
God, the Co-Heathens,
the Norse god Odin, King James,
The Big O, Sir Nick, and Mothlady Brittany.

And absolutely no thanks whatsoever to the assholes.